# THE BITTER WITHY

Also by Donald Revell

# THE
# BITTER WITHY

Donald Revell

Alice James Books

FARMINGTON, MAINE

10 9 8 7 6 5 4 3 2 1

Alice James Books are published by Alice James Poetry Cooperative, Inc., an
affiliate of the University of Maine at Farmington.

ALICE JAMES BOOKS
238 MAIN STREET
FARMINGTON, ME 04938

www.alicejamesbooks.org

Library of Congress Cataloging-in-Publication Data
Revell, Donald
The bitter withy : new poems / by Donald Revell.
    p.  cm.
ISBN-13: 978-1-882295-76-0
ISBN-10: 1-882295-76-5
I. Title.
PS3568.E793B58 2009
811'.54--dc22                    2009025413

Alice James Books gratefully acknowledges support from individual donors,
private foundations, the University of Maine at Farmington and the National
Endowment for the Arts. ❦

Cover art: Titian (Tiziano Vecellio) (c.1488-1576)
"Virgin of the Rabbit (Virgin and Child with St. Catherine)" Oil on canvas.
Location : Louvre, Paris, France
Photo Credit : Réunion des Musées Nationaux / Art Resource, NY

*for John Ashbery*

# Contents

## Acknowledgments

My thanks go to the editors of the following journals where many of these poems first appeared:

*American Poetry Review*: "Crickets"
*a side*: "Pine Creek"
*Barrow Street*: "The Land to which I Go," "A Painting of Cezanne's"
*Bombay Gin*: "Tools," "The Man with Beautiful Manners Gone"
*Caffeine Destiny*: "For Lucie"
*Conjunctions*: "The Rabbits," "Can't Stand It," "Spice," "Cambria,"
  "Kentucky"
*Court Green*: "Little Bees"
*Electronic Poetry Review*: "Butterfly," "Lullay My Liking"
*Free Verse*: "Nemesis," "Under the Railway Bridge in Albi"
*Gulf Coast*: "Days of Illness"
*Mipoesias*: "Lissen," "Comes to Me"
*New America Writing*: "Lay of Smoke," "Lay of Wood," "Lay of
  Waters"
*Poetry*: "Death," "Odysseus Hears of the Death of Kalypso"
*Quarterly West*: "Autumn Weave"
*Saranac Review*: "Flight"
*Slope*: "Desert Willow," "Drought," "Monterey"
*The Cincinnati Review*: "Roosevelt Island," "My Name Is Donald"
*The Laurel Review*: "West Agate"
*The Modern Review*: "Against This Quiet"
*Washington Square*: "The Bitter Withy"

Thanks also go to the University of Iowa's Center for the Book which printed a broadside version of my poem "Against Creation."

*What is our life without a sudden pillow—*
*What is death without a ditch?*

—Hart Crane

I

# TOOLS

Just at dawn the full moon
In its coin of rainbow
Called my name. I'd been cold,
Out walking the dog, while indoors
The children slept a little while longer.
And then I wasn't cold anymore.
I have a name, and it isn't a problem.

I have a soul, and it's no problem
To feel it slipping away from me
Into a name the full moon
Shouts to the sun.
A rainbow is as good a place as any.
Heaven's handy, and heaven's welcome
To my soul today.

# MONTEREY

A kindred mind with mine,
The sky has no idea, having
Gorged itself on diamonds.
Who put us here?
Who put us here with eyes?
I look at the sky. The sky looks down.
Saw yesterday three little birds,
Olive green above white breasts—
My father's birthday.
He is in heaven with his eyes.
When I was a child I was rain,
And he and God were all the clear,
Fragrant spaces and mind among mine.
The birds knew, and the rainbow too. I was looking.

# FLIGHT

Instance of emptiness—knowing
How is not knowing, e.g.
The enormous man selling
Over the airplane telephone while below us
An emptiness made of ten million stones
Of mist (or is it the sun haze,
The exhalation of a star in every stone?)
Prepares his soul and my soul
For heaven and for heavens.
It is 2004 and 140 A.D.
Juvenal's *Satires* find America.
*No cede malis*. We are killing
Everyone not here.
What better now to be than empty,
Than a star breathing size into mist?
Heaven. Heaven. Heaven. Heaven.
Rhymes with giving in.
Rhymes with given.

# CAN'T STAND IT

I hear the elephant music
Of the playground's rusted swings, and up,
Up higher, then down again,
Happy children take the sound.

No snakes can read.
Walking across the ocean,
Walking on flowers nowhere to be seen,
I walk on gold.
So says hummingbird. So said the fountain
As it filled with sand one day
When I wasn't looking and my son grew old.

Music dies with the man.
It dies surely, like a finger.
We have no poetry by William Blake.
Not a single note of Bach survives.
Stop kidding yourself.
Time is no river.
It is a shard of glass, cutting.

My Buddha in the wheelbarrow
Holds up a broken bottle while he's wheeled
Away. A diamond is a diamond.
A cloud is a cloud that looks like one.

In the afterlife,
I take my children to a playground.
Enormous birds perch safely on nothing.
The swings make no sound.

# SPICE

Pure green most pure
Among its own blue flowers,
Like rosemary, death
Is most itself when
Rooted at a threshold,
Playing at God by a gate
Until, when many years have passed,
The gate swings open, and death,
So carefully, with such
Small tremor, enters
The courtyard filled with children—
Phoebe, Benjamin, Caleb, Amy.
Oblivion is a child again.
Looking into its hands, it sees clouds
And then nothing.
Looking into my hands, I see clouds,
And they endure; they drift and endure.
One is broken glass. One is pure
Among its own blue flowers.

# AGAINST THIS QUIET

Or a haircut . . .
Hasn't the sky a yellow shirt, the sun,
Perhaps, torn where I saw a fog
Of humans and flowers, entity of a mirage,
Growing out of walls?
I'd come late to lateness.
I'd lost my little door and my low door.
We say "Mother has died" or
"How is it that she gave me what she never had?"
I mean happiness.
I mean a good Christmas.
Marrying detachment with respect,
Stray flowers to a nearby stranger's grave,
We stumble forward because only forward remains,
The white din up ahead.
I'd come late to lateness because mother forgave me.
And then she died.
Accents beyond any dream made a dream all day,
Every day,
As when a tree drops an arrowhead of leaf into your wine,
And the gaze of its standing
Repairs the sun too.

My dog is chasing a lizard.
In a dream, where the lizard isn't real,
He's screaming.
In the long way back out of sadness,
In new dark passages,
He accepts miter and tonsure.
That's not right.
The dog's really killed him.

Hasn't the sky a sky above it too?
When God prays, the sky turns blue.
Mother,
Even this crumb of life I also owe to you.
At the rainy cemetery, as my wife and children
Scrambled back into the limousine,
I felt I ought to stay, to
Be the branches of a tree
Forever for at least one day for Mother,
Eating the sky in all sincerity
Because she feared the sky,
And I'd come late.
I didn't stay.
Tell me, stranger, my only confidante,
Before the body is changed by the faces of evening,
Tell me I didn't stay.

# MY NAME IS DONALD

Like a fish on a hedge, the horsefly
Lands on my wife's lipstick.
That is sobriety.
That is the end of my hayride with oblivion.
I wonder: how long will it be until no one
Knows what a hayride is,
Or was? I've never been,
But the happiness I've seen in movies—
All the kids piled up in hay & a fiddler driving—
Is very real. It was real for a while.
Only a child can watch a movie sober.
He is younger than the mule pulling the wagon.
He is unshamed by the fiddler's expertise.
His birth trumps all, which is to say he's flying.

# NEMESIS

A man removes the animal from his eye,
And the animal dies—
Reluctant symmetry.
When I was alone I traveled
The entire way around the Earth on snow.
I was fast.

You were old.
Fleeing the sunken capital, almost naked,
You made your way to me. Sunlight
Sped us.
We rest now, unsteady but at rest,
On a broken parallel of white eucalyptus.

I saw the butterfly mating with a moth—
Reluctant symmetry.
I see
Parallel animals made from me.
They are sad in the shadows,
Happy when the sun escapes the tree.

# THE BITTER WITHY

Momentary wonder if more briefly now—
Themes, gardens tilted at the ecliptic
Where gardens go to die,
Black mountains beyond.
Mountains say the word.

Bicycle.
I am going to Europe.
Dear friend, take care of my bicycle for me.

Woodsmoke.
I will see woodsmoke
Riding bareback
The white ponies of Camargue.

Pigeon.
I never poisoned you.

# CRICKETS

## I

A canyon in the air,
A cloud to stand on:
I needed them,
And each, my Soul,
Like that mountain on the sun
You moved one good, strange day
Away from the fires
Into cold space,
Is past my strength.

## II

I was a boy dreaming I was a boy.
There were powers pressing me down
Into a cold place, and then
It was cold no longer.
Many colors of grass. Many trees.
My life unfolded there, fifty years and more;
And now, in cold rain, I'm the boy again,
Pressed down even harder than at first,
But with only dirt beneath me.

## III

My poor saint breaks the clouds
    Butter on a blue plate
    A dog beneath the table

My poor saint breaks the clouds
  What language is that
  What color

My poor saint breaks the clouds
  It is morning still
  The sky stays near

My poor saint breaks the clouds
  And each is a boy
  Each is dreaming

My poor saint breaks the clouds
  It being a good strange day
  And the ground is fires underneath me


IV


Where a cloud is tiger eyes upon the mountain
My death has daughters,
And one of them is mine.
In the climbing up, she'd grown yellow hair.
In coming down, it was white
Although, for one moment, it glowed
Brazen indigo in sunset light.

Only at the point of death
*Where my sunflower wishes to go*
*Where my sunflower wishes to go*
*Where my sunflower wishes to go*
Do the strong words
Tiger   Sunset   Indigo

Drive the whole weight of heaven like a single blade
   through the mind of man and through every mountain
   he has ever loved.


V


The rasp of motors teaching Chinese babies air guitar...
What is lovelier?
Nothing is lovelier, now it appears to me I'm dying,
Than crickets singing in broad daylight,
Eleven o'clock in the morning, a perfect
Indian summer day.

I read men in their faces, but God
I read in His creatures.
The creak of crickets, or is it only one?
No way to know, but only
After long and dear acquaintanceship with time
Does eternity come clear.
Only one cricket—just as I thought.


VI

*With that final detail of hair tossed from the window ...*
                                        —Barbara Guest

In the rough hewn entryway at Mesa Verde
Calling to the dog, to a strange dog
"Come home"—

If ever she steps out of that entryway
Into the full sunlight, my heart
Will leave my heart.
What happens then?

Snow in New York.
I'm trembling, it's
Minimal?
It's snow.
But this trembling, it's
Not minimal.
Paint it. Cricket. Cricket. Paint it.
It.
With that final detail of hair tossed from the window.


VII

I wrote my autobiography backwards
Years ago,
And in the white years since,
I've waited to be born.
It's always that way: catastrophe
Whitens all we are.
On the moving sidewalk at the Vatican Pavilion,
New York City World's Fair, 1964,
I passed *The Pieta* and was changed forever,
Seeing how very much younger
Mary was than was
Her murdered son.
God may be dangerous,
Better known by our not knowing.
Mary is nearer,
A little winter love in her white corner.
Mary is nearer,
And the cricket sits aside,
Chanting eternity like a lullaby to the murdered man
From roots of the white grass.

## VIII

I was a boy dreaming
I am a boy, I was,
I was dreaming,
And it's Christmas now;
And now is the time to turn
My poem, my Christmas,
Over to incendiaries.
Saint William Blake, pray for me;
Saint Rimbaud, pray for me;
Saint Antonin Artaud, burn
New eyes into my head
With a cigarette end.
Otherwise,
I am toys
Lost on the polar ice.

# ROOSEVELT ISLAND

Ever since his features have been gone,
My Buddha hides in the primroses.
God is shy of you. Now tell me,
Why are these hummingbird-moths,
In only May, so busy at midday?
Empty chair. Empty chair. Empty
Black folding chair falling backwards
Into the hollyhocks—whorish, blowsy things.
And then a bee arrives, so fat he's dripping with...
What is it? Pollen? Nectar?
Perhaps he is a rainstorm growing up from the ground.
30 years ago I drank some wine on an island.
My God is shy to tell you now:
Nothing's changed.

# BETWEEN STORMS

The rainbow seems to breathe
And so it breathes.

When it speaks it makes
The birds in our black trees

Glad and brave.

II

# FOR LUCIE

That would be bread.
That would be a table.
This is death, but it moves
Only one way;
And so the bread escapes,
And the table along with it,
Easily—as easily
As water spilling from a cup
All over the ground.

Now that I come to it,
Why agree to it?
Every quarter of the wind is bread.
Every blade of grass is a table.
We are walking beside deer through a halo.

# WEST AGATE

The disrepair is heavy,
Like one full day of summer, two months early.
Doves plod across the broken roof tiles. Who knows?
But flowers, small and purple where they shouldn't be,
Call to hummingbird, who never leaves us.
I've named him "Jesus." My son, who reads in the morning,
Calls her "Jill."

Music dies with the man.
Winter really is the end, but only one at a time.
And then the summer rushes in, lauding
The life's work, the legacy only now
Bursting into flower and flame.
Hummingbird has a dream without a name.
I know it.

# DESERT WILLOW

The yellowbirds will not come to a younger man.
And then you add the sky, creating trees
Which add their voices to the birds'.
Almost instantly, the sky falls down in flames.
Wait a moment. Take a drink. Brush
The fly from your wrist. Flesh falls away.
The bone becomes more slender, more attuned
To little changes in the wind, and then
The bone-branch flowers—soft trumpets
So quietly purple they are also white.
Welcome bees. Creation is something else.
I was living with good women from Italy
Right upstairs. The winter, after a long while,
Was a heavy bird, yellow where the sun would rise.

# LISSEN

There is a sound in birdsong
Just before the song,
And you can hear it,
Though only a few,
And those are reflected on lake water
    like beautiful ghosts
Always just at sunrise,
Do.

Tell the truth exactly, it will make
    no sense.
Click. Click.
Only a few, as in bowers.
Click. Click.
Only a few, as in a wedding party
    drowned in sight of the white lake shore.
Every church drives Christ into the weeds.
Earth is not old.

# LAY OF SMOKE

As if we were rabbits
All that's needed for our happiness
Is the end of the world

I woke this morning to a noise of strangers digging
A little grave for a little dog
Maxie
She belonged to Jeffrey my neighbor
A man with only one arm and a garden
Too big for this world

As if we were rabbits
All that's needed for any heaven
Is death and damage and a ditch
Covered with pine needles at the bottom
Into which goes the world

# LAY OF WOOD

Yellowbird here for one day only,
I'm telling you
The trees here
Are children of themselves. You can see it:
The deadwood in mid-air
Departing into mid-air,
And just below it,
Bright circles of emerald-green new growth.

The day is long when it is blind.
This morning, I find only darkness in me
Where yesterday I saw through countless eyes.

Yellowbird, I pray for change.
I dream about it,
The wild transformations,
Even as each day
The changes prove more terrible,
More set upon death and humiliation,
Even the humiliation of mountains.

I want celestial light, but not apocalyptic.
The end of the world is an old story.
I'm starting a new one.
Yellowbird here for one day only,
These emeralds are trees.
Fly fast.

# LAY OF WATERS

Once Christ, like a girl,
Held a buttercup under my chin.
Love fails.
A flower cuts my throat,
And angels weep from the wound—
Little angels.

Love never fails.
I met a woman in Kentucky.
There's no going back.
If I am in a woodland,
She is the woodland,
The warm, soft hand extended on the leaves.

A rill. A creek. A brook.
Whatever it is, we've come to it
In the catastrophe of little angels.
Leaves fall.
They catch fire, beautiful fire,
And never reach the ground.

Love fails and never fails.
Christ couldn't bear it, but *we* must.
We must walk on water and through a woodland too.
The actual past weeps from future wounds.
We have children,
And the children live on air.

# UNDER THE RAILWAY BRIDGE
# IN ALBI

Can you smell it,
Woodsmoke inside the camera?
A lost repose:
Stepping backwards into the photograph
I forget the garden waste on fire
Which is happiness, which becomes
Small snow falling across my world.
God lives.
God is the smoking perimeter
Of His eternal November.

In the photograph,
My hair is new and smells like fire.
I have forgotten the garden
Because I said so.

# AUTUMN WEAVE

Discarded gates,
Mountains of them,
And one tree—
What can I make of it
Sailing above the new fires
To an old life, my Eden
Of the low wall, the Holland
Sky, and Kennedy assassination?

The gated city is a salesman.
The heart has none, is no
Enclosure. Eyes and a mouth,
Eyes and a mouth always open:
Vision and the taste of garden
Words on the tongue.
The heart has none.

# COMES TO ME

Snow so very
Small so welcome,
A whited tree
Comes to me.

These are islands,
Imperiled generations
So very small
In their mid-air,
Mid-oceans of air.

Fever stirs in the snow.
My mother steps outside
Into 1919, and cold air
Closes her green eyes.
A glass breaks somewhere.

Small as snow,
Death is a window
Open at the beginning,
Open to the very end.

# THE MAN WITH BEAUTIFUL
# MANNERS GONE

Nothing remaining
Save only the image
Glimmering 30 years
In the trees
In deep shade
One pillar of sunlight
Embraces a leggy girl
Leaning a bicycle
On the one bright tree

Yellow bicycle
This is a message from the future

Yellow bicycle
This is protest and suicide by old means

Yellow bicycle
Take me

# FENCE LINE

I fell in love with wine,
A good horse for the girl
I loved and gave to another.
Cars go in sunshine. White fences
Run the entire length of hilly Pennsylvania.
Oceanic?
("Donald Revell's oceanic surrealism.")
Why not kill me?

I've said it before:
I write to postpone
The death of our hostess,
The girl I loved and gave to another.
Magic is sweet.
Magic survives until someone
Drives away with Yvonne.

# KENTUCKY

Ground-dwelling birds reply to thunder.
It is sunrise somewhere over there, while here
Stars shine still, and the secret doors inside the pines
Remain wide open. Which way to go?
When I walk into the sun, my children
Hurry beside me. I hear footsteps and machines.
When I go west into the stars, I see
Nothing I could show you: ghosts
Who are not ghosts at all, hearts
On their sleeves, eyes like melted diamonds.
I truly believe that someone loved me once.
A bird alighted on a bee alighting
On a green stem, and I heard thunder. God's favorites
Are the little stars He drops into the sun.

# A PAINTING OF CEZANNE'S

She turned the wheel. Immediately,
I was in the picture, coming home
To the angular house, to green boughs
Looming tenderly and massive.
Tenderness has mass, and Cezanne knew it.
Substance of a moment makes for substance.
Whatever lives at all, lives a long time.

She turned again, and the road
Shone bright, wide open all the way
We never went. Something was squandered.
As with eternal life and the love of God,
What makes actual human happiness
Nearly unbearable is its reality,
Its mass.

# THE RABBITS

I

After the soul of the flood
Let go its dream,
I let go mine.

Outside, the rabbits lived and died
As before, deep in the knowledge
Of stillness safely resting inside
Everything that moves
And in the medieval carpeting of clover.

I've seen apparitions since forever,
Domains I knew I'd someday enter
And never did. As a mourning child,
I marveled. As a bicycle rider, I sped
Through turns that did not bring me home.
The flood let go its dream.
Rabbits lived and died in clover.

II

How much would you give for one day's happiness?
I love the image of Christ's happiness when,
Still in his swathing clothes, he reached
To lay his hand upon the pure white rabbit
Mary held in her white hand for him.
The image is Titian's. The day was ending.
What did Christ pay?
                    Today in my garden,
I saw white feathers dangling in a spider's web

In bright sunlight. How much would you give
For one day's wings? My father changed a book
Into a house that flew. He died slow.
I think he wanted me to know that death
Was never mother to anything. Mary
Held a white rabbit in her white hand, knowing
Every child is born abandoned. All pay.


III


I knew a domain, a bicycle, and Denver.
I knew an abandoned child who was my mother.
Dead now. And so I know that beauty is a foundling,
A bicycle leaned against a disappearing tree.
Never once did I enter that green domain in Denver.
Morning after morning I rode faster and faster;
Always the trees disappeared. And then the house,
In a wink of an eye of a garden, would be gone.
I do not dream about it. There's no need.

In Titian's picture, in the background, a shepherd
Tends to a cluster of lambs. Not one of them
Is half so white as Mary's rabbit. Nor does the Christ child
See them. His hand is a counterweight
To the shepherd's hand. His gaze is a foundling
Abandoned in a disappearing tree.


IV


Mist white mountain fog and valley fog
Cool spaces
Like those between the letters of the names of stones
But no

---

I am not thinking of this earth nor seeking
Higher ground
I am watchful in these mists that quiet me
I am
A white gaze into a greater whiteness
Not seeking
Only waiting to see one face with eyes

*The smaller of two islands*
*The smaller of two islands*

Eyes of a foundling
Cloudbanks of white clover


V

A man once wrote a book about a lemon skin,
But I say
Nothing gets written.
Joys are creatures.
There are no books in the soul, only eyes
Meeting at the kitchen window at sunrise.

I make the coffee, and the rabbit watches me.
I rattle cups in the little basin, and he watches.
Something has driven all the predators from the sky.

From two islands,
You could make a city.
I know mine.
In all his life, a man loves only one,
And he does not choose it.
Mine is two islands, and I live on the smaller one.

"Make music," the rabbit says.
I cannot.
"Make the hawk's wings fold forever."
I cannot.
I can only tell you, although you are past hearing,
Christ's embrace of the woodlands hereabouts
Drove God out of the trees.


VI *The Vision of Saint Eustace*

In the antlers of a stag,
Christ on a cross-tree...
Have I one, if only one,
Conversion left in me?
My city is too far.
Islands are impossible
Because of empire, because of torturers,
Because not even drunkenness or prayer
Takes me the very little way
From murder to white clover.
God was driven out of the trees,
Taking shelter in a stag.
Not far, in the parched grass,
One rabbit fleeing one dog
Leaps.

# III

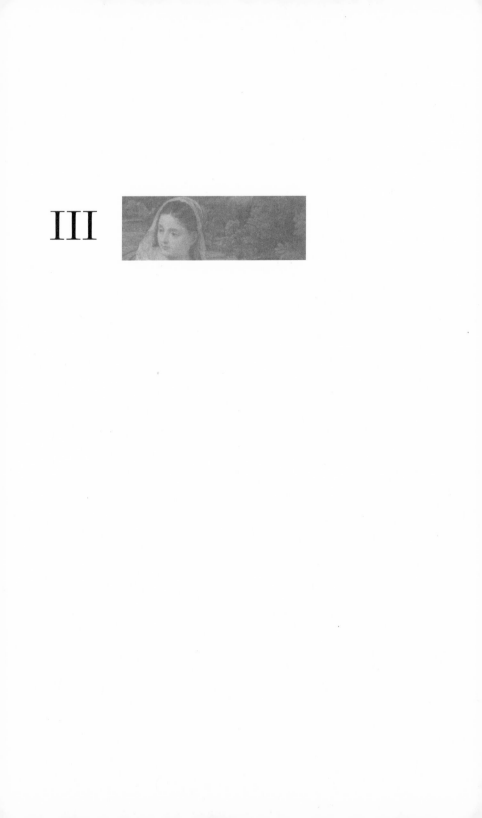

# AFTER ROUSSEAU

The mountains are nude
But not cold.

I shiver.
I believe in death
Now that death believes in me.

# AGAINST CREATION

Sovereign of my heart, your temple
Is deep in the dead branches,
Moving only when the wind
Delves so far.

Eden is ago.
I mean, all's terror now.
Sovereign of my heart,
I am shouting at nightfall:
Bats above me,
Hummingbirds skittish below the bats,
Almost like dragonflies.

I am shouting into debris.
Immodest happiness in Eden's humility—
Ago.
Ago.

Adam's fall invented the future.
He tied the bats' wings onto dragonflies.
Nature, even as it dies, abhors imagination.
What men call Extinction,
I call Home.

# DAYS OF ILLNESS

I can hear the rain 900 miles from here.
Nearer, two eyes open, vacant and pure,
Timelessness . . . there's no such thing. It would kill me.
I think of two small children, brother and sister.
They shelter small together beneath one tree.
Behind them, motionless in a rain-swept field,
Women in stiff, outdated clothing stand
Waist deep in the blowing grass. I would choose
To be the grass, to be moving, hoping
Somehow to draw the children's attention
And to draw them into the field. The women are dead
Long since. The children are old. The rain
900 miles from here is speaking through the grass,
From field to field to me so I might live.

# PINE CREEK

If I were better,
I'd push that little chair
More deeply into the honeysuckle,
Sit there and drink there, thinking
Only a moment ago
I was indoors, amazed
To be at home, my home, and seeing
So many white flowers in the window.

Only the one chair.
Is it because my dead are happy standing,
Perfectly at ease, each in his own flower?
Of course it is.
Yesterday, beside the path to Pine Creek,
I saw cactus flowers. In one, a bee
Waddled backwards into the sunlight.
He was fat with nectar, shining with it.
He'd have a dance to dance back home at the hive.
The dead were good to him.
The dead have been good to me.

# DEATH

Death calls my dog by the wrong name.
A little man when I was small, Death grew
Beside me, always taller, but always
Confused as I have almost never been.
Confusion, like the heart, gets left behind
Early by a boy, abandoned the very moment
Futurity with her bare arms comes a-waltzing
Down the fire escapes to take his hand.

"Death," I said, "if your eyes were green
I would eat them."

For what are days but the furnace of an eye?
If I could strip a sunflower bare to its bare soul,
I would rebuild it:
Green inside of green, ringed round by green.
There'd be nothing but new flowers anymore.
Absolute Christmas.

"Death," I said, "I know someone, a woman,
Who sank her teeth into the moon."

For what are space and time but the inventions
Of sorrowing men? The soul goes faster than light.
Eating the moon alive, it leaves space and time behind.
The soul is forgiveness because it knows forgiveness.
And the knowledge is whirligig.
Whirligig taught me to live outwardly.
Shoe shop . . . pizza parlor . . . surgical appliances . . .
All left behind me with the hooey.
My soul is my home.
An old star hounded by old starlight.

"Death, I ask you, whose only story
Is the end of the story, right from the start,
How is it I remember everything
That never happened and almost nothing that did?
Was I ever born?"

I think of the suicides, all of them thriving,
Many of them painting beautiful pictures.
I think of boys and girls murdered
In their first beauty, now with children of their own.
And I have a church in my mind, set cruelly ablaze,
And then the explosion of happy souls
Into the greeny, frozen Christmas Eve air:
Another good Christmas, a white choir.

Beside each other still,
My Death and I are a magical hermit.
Dear Mother, I miss you.
Dear reader, your eyes are now green,
Green as they used to be, before I was born.

# CAMBRIA

Games of ocean, games of trees, alarms.
The water is not for you.
The woodlands are too dense, and your heart
Will break before you find the clearings.
Keep to the vineyards.
The men there take their noonings;
Then comes heaven.
A vine speaks. It tells stories.
The dirt unfolds a music made at its birth,
Cool as the years, smooth as the lyre
God tunes in everything.
Of agony, I have nothing to say.
Of Cambria, a town where I was happy,
I say I never saw it, save at its best.

# LITTLE BEES

The dawn is a branch in my right eye.
What I need
Is not to look at all.
What I win
Is the Earth translated,
All its green things passing into blue.

Kids, I think of a cool shore almost always.
The little bees have gone to sleep.
Low suns glow in the river.
I am losing my days to them.
I miss the days, but not too much.
Wherever they go, they make a meadow.

I am for blueness. Unquestionable truth
Is blue as death, I believe, and a sweet thing.

# LULLAY MY LIKING

One cloud
One all alone upright
As one bright-harnessed angel
Breasting the New Year's wind
Was leading me
He said aloud
"Duty is horror"

Lullay my liking
Lay your body down
One thousand fifty palms
One thousand one hundred and fifty
Maids of Orleans
What I mean to say is that I know
Duty is horror

I have a thing in my breast
A child from impulse
A forest on whose skirt
Is not the earth
A redbird
God give him bright-harness
When he is born when he is dead

# DROUGHT

In the tree beside me,
Hummingbird growls at beetle,
A low drone,
And while I'm finding them,
Horsefly sneaks into my cup of wine.

Eyesight is nobody.
Perspective dies before it lives,
And it lives a long time after death

Like birdsong.

When I die, I will begin to hear
The higher frequency,
A whine, as though the moment were a lathe.
It will be a true lathe,
All my life spinning off from it.

# ODYSSEUS HEARS OF THE DEATH OF KALYPSO

All their songs are of one hour
Before dawn, when the birds begin.
I sing another.
In helpless midday, at the hour
Even sparrows have no heart to shrill
Comes news . . . suddenly, the unimaginable
Needs imagination and finds none.

Violet ocean only nothing.
Smoke of thyme and of cedar,
Ornate birds, nothing.
Even a god who came here,
Hearing a sweet voice,
Would find only old fires now,
Brittle in the blackened trees.

She was mast and sail. She was
A stillness pregnant with motion,
Adorable to me as, all my life,
I have hidden a cruel, secret ocean
In sinews and in sleep and cowardice.
She forgave me. Once, she wept for me.
Our child died then, and she is with him.

# BUTTERFLY

I will never see Mexico.
I'm staying with you.

The planet's warmer today,
And when I look away

The hare hares. The empty
Galaxy of his good eye

Overflows with talons.
See me. I am one

More flower.
Mexico is barely an hour

South by airplane.
I'll stay.

How would you ever breathe your last breath
Without these little wings of our death?

# LONG-LEGGED BIRD

I

I have a sweet house
Halfway to the top of fires
No one knows. A moth knows:
Fire is a door, a sudden portal.
He flies in, and what remains
Behind to burn is not moth,
Merely discernment.
Ophelia said as much to Hamlet
Who never knew.
Death is an element
Like water and like fire,
And there are many of them,
All doors. Drowning, we are
Done with wisdom, which is carried out to sea.
Burning, we leave old minds gone up in smoke.

In a sweet house halfway
To extinction, the air—let me
Try to explain—the air is made
Of souls of women and men,
All dancing. There's nothing to see.
Acumen and discernment, as much
As wisdom and wax wings, are no help.
You must breathe the dead to feel the dancing.
Despair is the bass line, earth and straw.
Everything else, when you breathe it,
Is ecstasy. I want to explain—tremolos
And squealings and then a high sound
Sweeten the little halfway house
Forever. I mean it just goes on forever,

As through the little portals children pour.
I keep a fiddle in my bones.
At night sometimes, the vibration
Of deep strings becomes a trembling.
I wake up frightened at first, seeing
The shiny cadres of my dreams
Dispersed into dark corners and thin air.
Then, gradually, fear subsides.
I am only the music that I am, and always
It leaves me. Ordinary ecstasy. A waking
From silly dooms of inwardness. Watch
A butterfly alighted on an iris.
When it flies away it bursts the flower,
Projecting its colors and infant textures
Upward and out until the horizon itself
Is one pure flower flying home.


II


Loving the fire,
Moth feels nothing to forgive.

Lifted out of the water
By a thousand strengths
Of flowers, Ophelia lives.

Forgiveness is a watercourse and conflagration
All around the world, a great adventure.

When I walk on ground
I walk on my bones, making music,
Or, rather, feeling the music
Making me.

Out of thin air
Into pure air,
Horizon calls me.


III


I am attending to ten accidents.
I am searching through the colors.
I am going home to Colorado with bombs.
I am bringing a plum tree and a cherry tree
For a new town, and when the avalanche
Has come and gone, I will put them in the ground.
I expect there to be dancing.
I expect there to be forgiveness on the epic scale.
I have wasted the effort of all flowers because
I expect there to be forgiveness on the epic scale.
I keep a little man inside my bones.
His fiddling makes my Chinese daughter smile.


IV


When did our sweet Jesus
Become the purview and bad pretext of jailers?
How did loving kindness
Come to devastate the world with wars?


V


Overhead, a long-legged bird
Circles my sweet house. I feel
He is waiting for me to join him,
To find real wings and rise out of my own mind
Into his air.

What would I find there?
Portals and invisible heavy traffic...
My mother as a baby, my father a cowboy,
My sister, finally, after so much heartbreak,
A girl.
The body travels inside the soul.
The body's a passenger.
This has nothing to do with Jesus
Though he is right here beside me.
He is unhurt.

Overhead, the long-legged bird
Departs at last. I'm staying.
My soul was kind enough to put me here,
Halfway to extinction with good wine
And a fine little house,
So here I stay.
Bones of mine,
Play no mournful melodies.
There is no harm in all the world, little man.
There is only happiness
On a lofty slope where it still snows.
I am breathing with my dead. I feel them dancing.

# THE LAND TO WHICH I GO

Creation is creation's mind.
Look no further than a leaf,
Designing itself in the sun's
    pleasure,
For intelligent design,
And praise God.

The good old phrase,
Like a wooden steeple walking,
    rings true:
*Praise God from whom all blessings*
    *flow.*
The word is *flow*—no effort
  at all, and no denying it.

The world creates itself,
And God is every motion of
    its pleasure.
Lose any, lose all of it.
The leaf breaks faith with the
    quiet branch, becoming a leaf.
What I remember of death was no such thing.

# Notes

"Against This Quiet"—This poem was composed for a special issue of *The Modern Review* honoring John Ashbery's poem "Clepsydra" and interweaves numerous phrases from that gentle masterpiece into its own elegiac pattern.

"The Bitter Withy"—The poem takes its title from a traditional English Christmas Carol, circa 1400. In it, the child Jesus goes out into the rain to "play at ball." He meets three lordlings and asks them to join him. They refuse, scorning his lowly status. And so Jesus builds a bridge of sunbeams. When the lordlings begin to cross it, Jesus drowns them. Their grieving mothers complain to Mary who spanks her son with a withy (willow) branch. Outraged, Jesus condemns the willow to be the only tree to rot from inside out: "Oh, the withy, it shall be the very first tree/That perishes at the heart!"

"Crickets"—Dedicated to the memory of Barbara Guest.

"Lay of Wood"—Dedicated to the memory of John Fowles.

"Under the Railway Bridge in Albi"—Dedicated to Jean Rochefort.

"The Rabbits"—Saint Eustace was a $2^{nd}$ century Christian martyr. Before his conversion, he was a Roman general named Placidus. While hunting a stag one day in the woods outside of Rome, he had a vision of Jesus crucified between the antlers of his prey. He was a Christian from then on. In the year 118 A.D., he and his wife and sons were roasted to death inside a bronze statue of a bull by the Emperor Hadrian. In 1969, the Roman Catholic Church removed Eustace from the calendar of saints, judging his legend to be "completely fabulous."

Recent Titles from Alice James Books

*Winter Tenor*, Kevin Goodan
*Slamming Open the Door*, Kathleen Sheeder Bonanno
*Rough Cradle*, Betsy Sholl
*Shelter*, Carey Salerno
*The Next Country*, Idra Novey
*Begin Anywhere*, Frank Giampietro
*The Usable Field*, Jane Mead
*King Baby*, Lia Purpura
*The Temple Gate Called Beautiful*, David Kirby
*Door to a Noisy Room*, Peter Waldor
*Beloved Idea*, Ann Killough
*The World in Place of Itself*, Bill Rasmovicz
*Equivocal*, Julie Carr
*A Thief of Strings*, Donald Revell
*Take What You Want*, Henrietta Goodman
*The Glass Age*, Cole Swensen
*The Case Against Happiness*, Jean-Paul Pecqueur
*Ruin*, Cynthia Cruz
*Forth A Raven*, Christina Davis
*The Pitch*, Tom Thompson
*Landscapes I & II*, Lesle Lewis
*Here, Bullet*, Brian Turner
*The Far Mosque*, Kazim Ali
*Gloryland*, Anne Marie Macari
*Polar*, Dobby Gibson
*Pennyweight Windows: New & Selected Poems*, Donald Revell
*Matadora*, Sarah Gambito
*In the Ghost-House Acquainted*, Kevin Goodan
*The Devotion Field*, Claudia Keelan
*Into Perfect Spheres Such Holes Are Pierced*, Catherine Barnett
*Goest*, Cole Swensen
*Night of a Thousand Blossoms*, Frank X. Gaspar

Alice James Books has been publishing exclusively poetry since 1973. One of the few presses in the country that is run collectively, the cooperative selects manuscripts for publication through both regional and national annual competitions. New regional authors become active members of the cooperative, participating in the editorial decisions of the press. The press, which historically has placed an emphasis on publishing women poets, was named for Alice James, sister of William and Henry, whose fine journal and gift for writing went unrecognized within her lifetime.

❧

TYPESET AND DESIGNED BY MIKE BURTON

PRINTED BY THOMSON-SHORE

ON 30% POSTCONSUMER RECYCLED PAPER

PROCESSED CHLORINE-FREE